SOFT SPOKEN SPELLS

Poems for Your Inner Witch

Nichole McElhaney

Do not be afraid to bare your teeth –
you were not brought into this world
covered in blood to become a
gentle, tamed thing.

And the moon said to me –

my darling daughter,

you do not have to be whole

in order to shine.

I want to believe Ophelia rose

from that watery grave

– spitting pearls and teeth –

hell-bent on strangling a kingdom

that overlooked the nocuous nature

of a wildflower girl.

Name your daughter Lilith

and tell her she belongs to no man.

Name her

Circe

Morgana

Hekate

Medusa.

Tell her names have power.

Tell her she's a force to be reckoned with.

My dear girl,

You should never have to hide parts of yourself

to keep the peace – you should never have to be

complacent in your own suffering.

When the world tries to silence you,

promise me you'll scream.

I have been "too much"

and I have been "not enough"

and then I realized

that the only opinion that matters

is mine.

I catch the first scent of spring in the air

and I know Persephone has returned

to her doting mother

and I have to admit,

I'm a little envious,

because I never had someone

bathe the world in flowers

to welcome me home.

I am tired of this thing I have become;

this woman-child who is all

burnt syllables and raw knuckles

with a heartbeat like a

war drum.

Tell your beasts

I have nurtured many a demon

and understand the taste for blood

better than anyone.

Aphrodite

What men call vanity, I call divinity.

What men call lust, I call power.

I was born of the sea

and I shall show

no mercy.

The crown you wear is not a decoration darling –

when push comes to shove,

show them who has the real power.

I think the women before me

carried a sorrow in their bones

that stretched

and stretched

and left me with an aftertaste

that I can't quite shake.

This museum of broken bone,

this cathedral of shattered teeth —

a place of worship and regret

where angels wear their sin

like a badge of honor.

I wanted to be the girl

with roses blooming on her tongue,

and that is when I learned

that speaking in flowers

means having to choke down thorns.

What am I

but a collection

of sins

wrapped in

frailty.

I am not ashamed of this blood

that flows like honey –

this reminder that I am ripe

with possibility

and promise.

There's a revolution brewing

in my veins

and all the fires you light

can never lick the hemline

of this witch.

She is the type of girl

who eats belladonna

because her mother always told her,

"you are what you eat",

and she longs to be the kind of beauty

that is capable of so much

ruin.

A poem is an offering

of heavy tongue and

blistered finger and

thickened blood –

it is a gesture and

a surrender and

a longing to be more

than our mortality allows.

Hades

I was crafted from this darkness —

this ancient womb.

I do not fear silence, emptiness;

it is from these sacred seeds

that life, and light, are born.

Medusa

There are some who say

that the stripping of my beauty was a curse.

Others will tell you it was a gift.

Athena is painted as jealous or benevolent.

I am painted as victim or harlot.

No one ever mentions Poseidon,

whose damnable deed led to this tragedy.

Artemis

Arrows and blood and shadows

chasing

chasing

chasing

I am a war cry tumbling

from the mouth

of a child.

Dear girl with your thighs dripping honey,

you are the moon incarnate.

Let yourself unfold like a rose:

perfume sweet and red as sin.

I whisper all my secrets to the moon;

she understands the magic

of living in shadows.

I stitched my broken heart back together

with barbed wire.

It's the most lethal part of me now.

It's ok if the garden you planted

inside of yourself has begun to whither;

we cannot always be in bloom.

But please, keep watering

and pruning

and tilling the soil –

be resilient,

and you will flourish again in time.

There was a time, long ago, when all the crows

knew my name.

And magpies would gather round

to hear the spells I would weave.

But somewhere down the road,

the magic started to fade,

and now all those black birds sit and weep for me.

I twist and turn within these bones –

a changeling walking a tightrope

of spider's silk

woven between this world

and the next.

They counted on the sirens to lose their voices,

the harpies to lose their claws,

but we will rise like phoenixes

and burn them to the ground.

(your time is up)

Alchemistress

There is no greater power

than that of a woman

who has learned to turn salt water

into flame.

They turn girls like us

into monsters

then come for us with

pitchforked tongues.

I am tired of carrying these ashes around

from the flame that used to burn

between us.

I have pressed my fingertips

against the darkness long enough

to know the tangibility

of sorrow.

Imagine: a girl so hungry for love,

she soaks up kindness

like a flower soaks up sunlight.

Here I lay –

bare breasted and sanctimonious:

a martyr steeped

in wickedness.

There is no honey

on these palms of mine –

only thorns ripped from roses

too embarrassed to bloom.

One day you will meet a boy

who will call you a mermaid

and you will learn

that his pretty words mean nothing

if he doesn't believe in

your magic.

I no longer apologize

for all the parts of myself

that you didn't know how

to love.

Don't ever let anyone fool you into thinking

you must scorch your insides

by swallowing all the words

they're too afraid to hear.

(always speak your truth)

The day is coming

when you will read my words

and feel the heat behind every syllable

and realize you're not as

fire proof

as you thought.

Take note of the girls who run with wolves:

they know the value of their wildness.

Hecate

To be called crone

is somehow frowned upon –

but truth be told –

they fear my knowledge,

my magick,

my ability to peer into the darkness

and not flinch at what

stares back.

I delight in the heavy silence

of your absence.

Here in the dark,

we do not mourn monsters.

She emerges from the gloom

under the protection of a blood moon,

secrets etched upon her palms,

spells brewing in her rosebud mouth.

What does a girl do

when she is born with a sharp mouth,

a tongue that drips battle cries,

a heart that turns fear into fire?

She becomes a champion for the weak,

a voice for the broken.

She becomes you.

She becomes me.

I may be full of darkness

but I am also full of hope,

and like Pandora,

you'll find I am impossible

to resist.

Not everyone will know how to handle you,

but you were not made for others.

Never be afraid

to be your own kind of storm.

My body is not a temple,

for temples turn to ruin and rubble.

My body is a forest

of bramble and thorn and hemlock.

I will not fade;

I will devour.

Even Atlas wasn't burdened

with as heavy a weight

as the one you laid

upon my shoulders.

I built my throne

from the wreckage

you left behind

and now it's your turn

to get on bruised knees

and beg.

A floral tomb for a dark queen;

an underworld of whispers and ruin;

this is where I dwell –

this is where I burn.

Do not judge others

for how they choose

to wear their crown.

There is no wrong way to be a queen.

I am drawn to things that glitter in the dark.

Like a magpie,

I collect them and keep them

close to my heart.

The snow melts,

taking your memory with it.

There is no room for you here

in my blossoming spring.

Mother,

how do I explain

that he is softer than any petal

growing in your garden?

Mother,

how do I show you

that I can make spring bloom

in the darkest parts of him?

Mother,

how can I convince you

to let me go?

- Persephone

My mother strung rowan berries

around my throat,

stitched a four leaf clover

onto my skirt,

laid a witch's kiss upon my brow –

but she's never met a creature like you,

and all the charms in the world

couldn't keep me from falling

under your spell.

I am a girl enchanted –

a fairytale made flesh and bone.

I think of all the girls I used to be:

the one who didn't survive

the big bad wolf,

the one who never woke

from her enchanted sleep,

the one whose heart

resides in a wooden box.

I hope they are resting easy now

with the knowledge that at least one of us

got a fairytale ending.

I am a cathedral full of crows

who cry triumphantly in the velvet twilight.

Listen.

Listen.

Hear the beating of their wings

against flesh and bone.

See their blue-black blush nestled

in my hollows.

Icarus

Did you really think that clipping my wings

would keep my from flying?

The men who write myths tell us

that Persephone did not seek the darkness;

they do not want us to know

that women can wield their power,

can claim a crown,

can demand to be called

Queen.

Learn to recognize

the slumbering wolf in others –

this is how you find your pack.

All of this ash on my tongue

tastes like redemption.

(we burn, and then we rise)

I am not a rose

doomed to bloom

for a beast

of a man.

(cultivate your own magic)

Some days I hold my heart

between my teeth

and let everyone see

all the bloody truths

I carry.

I walk the kingdom of Hell

planting seeds of hope

and wait for my salvation

to be ripe for harvest.

I have been digging this grave

since the day I crawled –

wretched and ruined –

from the ashes of my resurrection.

Do not speak to me of death,

for I have long been fluent

in the serpent's tongue.

I do not forgive you

for the way you hurt me –

but I do forgive myself

for believing my love

could turn a monster

into a man.

I didn't crawl through the flames of hell

so that you could write a poem

about how beautiful it is

to be broken.

(my tragedies are not your muse)

Sometimes I find my Gods tucked away

like a favorite toy left in an attic;

I take them out

and dust them off

and promise to treat them better.

I never do.

(we abandon what abandons us)

I will weave serpents in my hair

and perfect a nightmare stare

and you will call me hideous,

but at least I won't have to suffer your gaze twice.

(my "ugliness" is armor)

I can hold the darkness in the palm of my hand,

breathe it in like dust,

and let it settle over my bones.

I can be the thing you fear

when the moon is void

and all the stars have dissolved

into nothing.

I can teach you that death, too, can be a gift.

I have built my kingdom in a garden of serpents;

they have named me queen

and crowned me

with sin.

Morrigan

She is a sharp tongue dripping war;

a battle cry cloaked in shadow.

She speaks in devastation,

her accent laced with blood.

Persephone

I have tasted death:

ripe fruit and salvation.

I have tasted death –

and I have come for its crown.

Let us arm our daughters

with tender hearts

and sharp teeth;

let us teach them that the world,

though cruel,

will not be their undoing.

Sleeping Beauty

Honeyed webs spun behind

violet lids

A tangle of briar to cradle

golden limbs

A spindle, a kiss, and a kind blue fairy's gift

How many men have told you

that your body is a temple

that should be kept sacred and pure?

How many of those men

then scolded you

for not opening your doors

and welcoming

their sacrilege?

(my gods devour deceivers)

And I will consume the moon's shadow

if it helps me achieve

divinity.

Slipping through the forest

with salt upon my feet,

I leave a golden trail

and a prayer tangled in the leaves:

find me

find me

find me

I don't run with the wolves –

I lead the pack.

The roses are still blooming.

No one told them summer is ending.

No one wants to be left

with only an offering

of thorns.

Like a spider in a web,

I notice the tiniest ripples.

I am patient.

I am swift.

I am fangs

and silk

and I spare no one.

(be careful where you tread)

I am a girl made of ash

and smoke

and singed edges.

How silly of me to believe

anyone could find beauty

in a burning house.

Unsung prayers,

honey thick,

stick in my throat.

Divinity tastes like a promise –

floral and sweet with a hint

of venom.

These bones of mine house a goddess

and never again shall she be mistreated.

I am the clutter in your dreamcatcher,

the shadow creeping in your peripheral,

the tapping of nails against

darkened windowpanes.

I am the reminder that around here,

your dead never stay buried for long.

If I must go,

then it shall be in a final blaze

of glory.

(even a phoenix runs out of lives)

Made in the USA
Middletown, DE
07 December 2020